MW01294924

Creative Therapy in the Sand

Using sandtray with clients

Roger & Christine Day

Brook Creative Therapy

Copyright © Roger & Christine Day 2012

First published in 2012 by
Brook Creative Therapy

All rights reserved. No part of this publication may be
reproduced or transmitted in any form or by any
means, electronic or mechanical, including
photocopy, recording or any information storage and
retrieval system, without permission in writing from
the publisher. Pages may be photocopied for
therapeutic, supervisory and training use only.

Published by:

Brook Creative Therapy, Brook Cottage, 16 Burnside,
Rugby, Warwickshire CV22 6AX, UK

Details of how to order further copies can be obtained
by emailing brookcreativetherapy@gmail.com

About the authors

Roger Day

Certified Transactional Analyst, Psychotherapist and Play Therapy specialist

For many years Roger has been a trainer and supervisor specialising in children and families. Now retired, he lives in Rugby, Warwickshire.

Christine Day

European Adult Teaching Certificate, Nursery Nurse Examination Board (NNEB), Diploma in Counselling, Certificate in Counselling Skills

Christine is a qualified nursery nurse. In addition to successfully raising four children, over the years she has added play and creativity specialisms to her nursery skills. Christine lives with Roger in Rugby, Warwickshire.

Books by Roger & Christine Day:

Matryoshkas in Therapy: Creative ways to use Russian dolls with clients
Creative Anger Expression
Creative Therapy in the Sand: Using sandtray with clients

Christine & Roger Day have also published the following books in CD-ROM form:

Body Awareness: 64 bodywork activities for therapy (2008/2011)
Therapeutic Adventure: 64 activities for therapy outdoors (2008/2011)
Stories that Heal: 64 creative visualisations for use in therapy (2011)

Brook Creative Therapy, Brook Cottage, 16 Burnside, Rugby CV22 6AX, UK

Acknowledgements

Being parents four times over and now having three grandchildren has been the best way for us to learn how toys and other small objects can be grouped together to create whole worlds in miniature. Add some sand and – voila! – a sandtray is created.

More formally, Roger is very grateful to the late Dr Jim Stringer for introducing him to Carl Jung's unconscious process, a vital part of sandtray therapy.

Trainers John Daly and Monika Jephcott provided formal training for us in using sandtray in a wide variety of contexts, including sandtray without objects and differences in sandtray work for children and adults, males and females.

Above all, we are grateful to child and adult clients as well as trainees and supervisees for their insight and ideas that have made this book such a rich and varied resource.

Introduction

Sandtray is a powerful therapy involving the client placing small objects in the sand within a box, the base of which is coloured light blue. This is a definition of sandtray therapy at its simplest. More complex is that sandtray therapy involves working intuitively, usually at an unconscious level, and often results in actual therapeutic changes in the client engaged in the sand.

The roots of sandtray go back over 100 years, not to a psychologist or psychiatrist, but to author and science fiction writer H G Wells (1866-1946). In the room where Wells did his writing he kept a range of small toys. Breaking with the formal conventions of the Edwardian era, Wells would get on the floor with his two small sons and together create imaginary worlds. In 1911, when son George was 10 and his brother Frank was eight, Wells published the book *Floor Games* about these activities.

After explaining the type of toys he and his sons used, he writes: 'These we arrange and rearrange in various ways upon our floor, making a world of them. In doing so we have found out all sorts of pleasant facts, and also many undesirable possibilities; and very probably our experience will help a reader here and there to the former and save him from the latter' (Wells, 1911).

Later, when therapists identified the effectiveness of this world in miniature and a sand box was added, the focus was on therapy with *children.* It is interesting to note that here Wells as an adult includes himself in finding out 'pleasant facts' and 'undesirable possibilities'. Today sandtray therapy is equally as successful with adults, couples and families as it is with children.

In 1929, recalling her childhood enjoyment in reading *Floor Games,* British-born paediatrician and child psychiatrist Dr Margaret Lowenfeld (1890-1973) developed what came to be known as the Lowenfeld World Technique. She produced toys from her 'wonder box' along with trays of sand and the children at her clinic created their own miniature worlds from them.

She writes: 'My own endeavour in my work with children is to devise an instrument with which a child can demonstrate his own emotional and mental state without the necessary intervention of an adult either by transference or interpretation, and which will allow of a record being made of such a demonstration. My objective is to help children to produce something which will stand by itself and be independent of any theory as to its nature' (Lowenfeld, 1979/1993, page 3).

In 1937 Lowenfeld demonstrated her technique at a conference in Paris attended by Dr Carl Jung who seemed impressed with it. Interestingly, in 1912 Jung himself had created a world in miniature made up of rocks and stone from the lake shore in Bollingen, Switzerland, as part of his own healing following his painful break from Sigmund Freud. With Jung's encouragement, Dora Kalff (1904-1990), a family friend and neighbour in Switzerland, began training in psychoanalysis. When she had completed her study in 1949 she began to adapt Lowenfeld's World Technique to Jungian therapy. She called her new technique 'sandplay therapy'.

Right up to the present day the term 'sandplay therapy' is used exclusively for therapy with a Jungian or post-Jungian model. All other models of therapy use the alternative term 'sandtray therapy'. This book focuses on sandtray therapy using a theoretical model based mainly (though not exclusively) on transactional analysis (TA). It seems useful to give the wider picture of the development of therapy in the sand before introducing some TA thoughts.

Sandplay therapists hold strongly to their belief that the Jungian approach is the best – even the only – way. In her excellent book *The Handbook of Sandplay Therapy,* Barbara Turner states that the book takes 'a specifically Jungian approach to the material. The reason for this is that the Jungian approach to the work allows for the deepest order of psychic transformation' (Turner, 2005, page 1). Another excellent author, Ruth Ammann, also takes the view that Jungian and sand techniques are meant for each other. 'I believe that classical dream analysis and sandplay belong together,' she writes. 'They represent two equally valid therapeutic approaches which allow us to adapt better to the psychological needs of the analysand [client]. Both methods are founded on the psychology of C G Jung' (Ammann, 1991, page xv). Lois Carey, who pioneered sandplay therapy with families, writes: 'The ability to understand the archetypal level of the psyche through Jungian sandplay enables deeper healing to occur than is possible when other theoretical bases are employed' (Carey, 1999/2008, page 11).

Despite these exclusivistic claims, those of us using other models with sandtray therapy find that this technique works just as well. Most of the approaches to sandtray have emerged from the development of play and play therapy. Melanie Klein and Anna Freud (daughter of Sigmund Freud) introduced play into the therapy room in their work with children. Virginia Axline later took these ideas, along with the nondirective approach of her mentor Carl Rogers, and developed play therapy.

In her original post-war book Axline writes: 'Nondirective play therapy grants the individual the permissiveness to be himself; it accepts that self completely, without evaluation or pressure to change; it recognises and clarifies the expressed emotionalised attitudes by a reflection of what the client has expressed; and, by the very process of nondirective therapy, it offers the individual the opportunity to be himself, to learn to know himself' (Axline, 1948/1974, page 15).

While in 1948 Axline makes no mention of sand in the therapy room, in her later and better-known book *Dibs: In search of self* (Axline, 1964/1990) she refers to her young client's nondirective exploration of self through putting objects in the sandbox.

According to Janet West the play therapist's role in sandplay 'is to observe and to support but to avoid interfering or making suggestions. As in other aspects of play therapy, sometimes the play therapist may ask amplifying questions, or invite the child to tell a story about the sand picture.

Interpretation is unnecessary and would only rarely be offered' (West, 1992, page 75).

Probably the best-known play therapy style outside of a nondirective approach is that of Gestalt therapist Violet Oaklander. This takes a largely here-and-now approach, looking at the phenomenology of therapy in the sand and the projections emerging from it.

Oaklander writes: 'When a child makes a sand scene, draws a picture, or tells a story, he is tapping into his own individuality and experience. Often these expressions are metaphorical representations of his life. When he can own aspects of these projections, he is making a statement about himself and his process in life. His awareness of himself and his boundaries intensifies. When the child describes his safe-place drawing to me, he feels heard and respected as I listen carefully. When I ask him to give me a statement about his place that I can write on his picture, he feels further validated. When we connect his statement to his life today, he begins to feel his own significance in the world' (Oaklander, 1997, pages 300-301).

Another approach is that of cognitive behavioural play therapy. Susan Knell, while stressing the importance of being aware of developmental issues in children, writes: 'The cognitive model is based on the interplay between verbal processes and behaviour. Building on the model, cognitive therapy is largely verbally based, with the client working with the therapist to identify cognitions and test the validity of personal thoughts, assumptions and beliefs' (Knell, 1995, page 73).

Sandtray using TA combines many of these approaches, enabling clients to make autonomous decisions in their Adult ego state ('nondirective'), present-centred redecisions ('own aspects of these projections') and engage in the process of decontamination ('test the validity of personal thoughts, assumptions and beliefs'). For a full theoretical understanding of these and other TA concepts included in this book we recommend reading *TA Today: A new introduction to transactional analysis* (Stewart & Joines, 1987).

While TA still embraces the four 'pillars' of life-script, games, ego states and transactions, in the last three decades it has shifted its focus in line with other therapy models. Heather Fowlie writes: 'In TA, there has been a move away from a focus on cognitive insight as the primary means of psychological change to the importance of affective, cocreative, conscious, nonconscious and unconscious relational interactions as a primary means of growth, change and transformation' (Fowlie, 2010).

Sandtray using TA aims to work relationally, taking account of transference and countertransference. It also looks at conscious, unconscious and nonconscious processes. Thus it combines focus on the relationship with the client and a return to some of TA's psychoanalytical roots.

One way of understanding this approach to sandtray is to think of an iceberg. The 10 per cent of the iceberg above the surface represents the client's *conscious thinking, feeling, behaviour and attitude.* Then there is an area just at the water's surface that is sometimes revealed by the waves and sometimes is under the water. In TA we call this the client's *out-of-awareness* or *nonconscious.* The rest of the 90 per cent of the iceberg below the surface is the *unconscious.*

In 'talking' therapy counsellors work mainly with the conscious, drawing on the nonconscious whenever possible, helping to bring into conscious awareness what may be partially hidden. The aim of doing this is to influence the unconscious, enabling clients to make redecisions.

In therapy using sandtray clients work directly with the unconscious, hopefully drawing on the nonconscious, in order to make changes that affect their conscious thinking, feeling, behaviour and attitude.

This process in sandtray therapy has a parallel with night-time dreams. Dreams are the brain's natural way to sort out our thinking (or, in computer-speak, defragment the hard disk). In the same way, sandtray helps clients intuitively to sort out their emotional difficulties. That is why it is vital not to interpret what the client creates. Instead, the therapist validates, supports and gives feedback.

In TA terms this sorting out of emotional difficulties is called a script change or redecision. Eric Berne, founder of TA, introduced to the therapy world the concept of life-script. He defined this as 'an ongoing life plan formed in early childhood under parental pressure. It is the psychological force which propels the person toward his destiny, regardless of whether he fights it or says it is his own free will' (Berne, 1972/1975a, page 52). Stewart & Joines (1987) refine this definition as 'an unconscious life-plan made in childhood, reinforced by the parents, "justified" by subsequent events, and culminating in a chosen alternative' (page 330).

As children we make our own script decisions at an unconscious or nonconscious level as the best way we know at the time for responding to the world around us. Those script decisions were useful at the time but some of them now restrict our clients in their relationships, emotions and attitudes to life.

Therapists using sandtray with clients observe the process, being aware of any emotions that arise in themselves. They consider any intuition they have as the client works in the sandtray. By verbalising their transferences and countertransferences as well as any intuition they have, the client is helped towards making script changes.

Before he developed TA Eric Berne spent considerable time and resources in exploring and writing about intuition. Indeed, some people have suggested that Berne developed TA in order to understand the power of intuition.

Berne gives the following definition: 'Intuition is knowledge based on experience and acquired through sensory contact with the subject, without the "intuiter" being able to formulate to himself or others exactly how he came to his conclusions. Or in psychological terminology, it is knowledge based on experience and acquired by means of preverbal unconscious or preconscious functions through sensory contact with the subject' (Berne, 1949, page 203).

It was Berne's belief that intuition was a missing element in the psychological processes of his day. He writes: 'To understand intuition, it seems necessary to avoid the belief that in order to know something the individual must be able to put into words what he knows and how he knows it. This belief, still common since Freud, is the result of what appears to be an overdevelopment of reality testing which tempts some who are interested in psychology to think too far away from nature and the world of natural happenings' (Berne, 1949, page 223).

Counsellors often focus only on a person's thinking, rational self. Sandtray therapy redresses the balance by emphasising a client's nonverbal, nonrational self. Popular writer Malcolm Gladwell, in *Blink,* his excellent book on intuition, writes that 'if we are to learn to improve the quality of the decisions we make, we need to accept the mysterious nature of our snap judgments. We need to respect the fact that it is possible to know without knowing why we know and accept that – sometimes – we're better off that way' (Gladwell, 2005, page 52).

Because it is mysterious, sandtray has often been associated with new age, mystical philosophies and minority religious belief systems. In this book we take a more down-to-earth approach based on intuition. Part of this intuition involves observing tiny changes in clients' face and body while they are working in the sand. These changes combine to form what in Gladwell's view we perceive as intuition. By combining our observations with our own intuitive feelings and thinking we can give feedback to clients in their journey towards change.

Once the sandtray and objects have been gathered (see next section 'Getting started'), there are several steps to effective sandtray therapy with clients. First, consider whether your client needs to work with some direction from you or entirely nondirectively. This book contains several ideas for giving direction to clients that have been shown to be effective. An excellent guide to directive/nondirective and conscious/unconscious processes in sandtray therapy and other play therapy techniques is *Play Therapy Dimensions Model* (Yasenik & Gardner, 2004/2012).

Make sure that the sand is smooth in the sandtray to give clients a 'blank canvas' to work with. You can do this by hand as we do or, if you prefer, you can use a ruler or piece of wood to get a really smooth surface.

Then consider how you will position yourself in relation to the client. You could sit where you normally sit in the therapy room and let the client move around the sandtray. More common is to move with the client, sitting or standing near while the client places objects. You could sit opposite the client, to one side or (our current favoured approach) alongside the client while he or she works in the sand.

Next, what do you say while clients are working in the sand and when they have finished? Our strong recommendation is to avoid interpretation. Instead, comment on what the client is *doing* and give your intuitive *thinking* and *feeling*.

In terms of comments on what the client is doing, avoid naming an object. When you see the client putting soldiers beneath the sand you might say something like: 'You seem really determined to bury those objects.' The word 'soldiers' is not used. They could represent something completely different.

Use your own intuition in terms of thinking and feeling. For instance, if you notice the client placing objects angrily you could say something like: 'You seem really angry when you're putting those objects in the sandtray.' This can be done by noticing tiny changes in the client's face, voice and body position. It has a parallel with recognising ego states.

The idea of ego states – Parent, Adult and Child – was one of Eric Berne's best-known concepts. An ego state has been defined as 'a consistent pattern of feeling and experience directly related to a corresponding consistent pattern of behaviour' (Stewart & Joines, 1987, page 329). Berne identified five ways of recognising ego states through a person's behaviour:

❏ Words
❏ Tones
❏ Gestures
❏ Postures
❏ Facial expressions

Watch for the clues in these areas, combine them with your own transferential reactions and you have some tools to work with clients in sandtray therapy. When clients say they have finished creating a sandtray ask if they are sure they are finished. Make absolutely sure they are finished before moving on.

A client does not need to create a sandtray in every session. Indeed, people who call themselves sandtray or sandplay therapists often have several talking sessions between each sandtray.

Remember to photograph each sandtray when it is complete. Ideally pictures should be without flash because the bright light tends to change the colour of the objects and hide some objects behind shadows. It is best to take the picture from the same direction the client faced when he or she did the sandtray. This will highlight eye positions and give a general 'feel' of the whole tray as the client saw it. The picture becomes part of the client's notes. It is also useful if the client wants to recreate the same sandtray next time.

Finally, whether you are brand new to sandtray or an experienced practitioner, learn from your mistakes, attend regular training so that you can experience work in the sand yourself and, above all, enjoy the power of creative therapy in the sand.

Getting started

Sandtrays

Sandtrays come in many shapes and sizes. Some experts believe that only one size and shape – 72.0 cm (28.5 inches) long x 50.0 cm (19.5 inches) wide x 7.5 cm (3.0 inches) deep – is suitable. This is based on the belief that this is the ideal size to see the sandtray out of the corner of the eye while watching the client's facial expressions. We believe it is important that you find a size and shape (even round) that suits your work with clients. Whatever size you choose, it is essential to have blue at the bottom to represent sea, water or rivers. One option is a plastic school tray sprayed with blue. Another is to buy a ready-made sandtray from a play therapy supplier. You can use a drawer that slides under the bed, though the weight of sand will hinder the wheels moving. You could also make your own. Half fill your sandtray with play sand (see below). Expect your sandtray to have water put in it. Some therapists use a wet sandtray and a dry one so that the client only puts water in the wet one. Even with silicone sealing it is advisable to have a plastic cloth under the sandtray.

Sand

Play sand is available from large toy suppliers, garden centres and DIY stores. It is important that it is nonstaining. Some therapists disinfect sand or objects from time to time. If you believe this is necessary that's fine.

Objects

You can spend a lot of money on objects for use in sandtray. We suggest you keep things simple. You will need: people; cars and other machines; wild animals and domestic animals; natural objects from the woods or the beach; monsters; symbolic items; religious objects; beautiful items; and plenty of inanimate objects such as bridges, houses and plastic trees. Sometimes even broken things (a broken man or a piece of balloon) can have huge significance to the client. Then look in drawers and toolboxes at home. Choose objects that move such as a hinge, a nut and bolt or an old ratchet screwdriver. Choose your own collection of objects that suit you as a therapist. The items that symbolically mean something to you can become treasures for clients who need them to resolve difficulties.

How I want to be

Much of counselling and psychotherapy focuses on clients' difficulties. This sandtray changes the focus to a future that is bright for clients.

Invite clients to create in the sandtray how they would like to be when all their current difficulties are sorted out. Say that they don't need to explain what they are doing. Just use intuition. If they get stuck prompt them with phrases such as: 'Imagine yourself free of problems. Show how that would feel.' 'Create in the sandtray a future when you are free from those difficulties you face.'

An alternative is for clients to use objects to show where they have come from in life and where they are now. Discuss this together if the client wants to. Then ask: 'Where do you see yourself in six months? Use more objects if you would like.'

Once clients have created their sandtray, invite them to talk about their sandtray. If necessary prompt with questions such as: 'Looking at your sandtray how does it feel?' 'What do you think it will be like for you?' 'What will you do differently then?' You are looking here not for a logical explanation but for an intuitive response.

If appropriate, celebrate together the goal seen in the sandtray as if it has already been achieved in the client's life.

Theory

This activity could be seen as a form of positive psychology such as that developed by Solution-Focused Brief Therapy (SFBT), founded by Steve de Shazer and Insoo Kim Berg. SFBT 'assumes that all clients have some knowledge of what would make their life better, even though they may need some (at times, considerable) help describing the details of their better life and that everyone who seeks help already possesses at least the minimal skills necessary to create solutions' (ISFT, 2012).

Another way of looking at this is in terms of establishing a contract for change. A contract in TA terms is an 'explicit bilateral commitment to a well-defined course of action; an Adult commitment to oneself and/or someone else to make a change' (Stewart & Joines, 1987, page 328). The way a mere wish by a client can be transformed into a contract for change is by the therapist and client agreeing their parts in achieving the goal.

According to Ian Stewart (Stewart, 1996), a therapeutic contract uses positive words and has the following elements:

❒ It is based on actions.
❒ It is sensory based (the result can be seen, heard etc).
❒ It is finishable.

If you are working with a child, a sandtray such as this may be the only effective way to establish a treatment contract.

My family

A useful activity for many clients is to invite them to symbolise their family in the sandtray.

They could create their family of origin or, for adults, their present family. Sometimes clients find it difficult to portray each family member exactly using small people from the therapy resources. It makes sense, therefore, to suggest they create their family using, for instance, natural objects, animals or vehicles. In that way the family members will be portrayed more by characteristics than appearance.

Remember the golden rule of sandtray therapy when a client asks what an object is: 'It can be whatever you want it to be.'

When clients have finished invite them to talk about the family they see in the sandtray. Note the kind of objects chosen and their relationship to the actual people referred to.

A useful question to ask for this and other sandtrays is: 'If you were in the sandtray, where would you be?' Often clients will leave themselves out but they usually know intuitively where they would have been.

It is important for clients to know that they can only change themselves, not the rest of the family. Focusing on the object (or space) representing the client, ask: 'How could this object be moved so that the family works better?' If clients are willing, invite them to move this particular object. Then ask: 'What is that like now as you look at the sandtray?'

Be prepared for plenty of emotion in this activity. Exploring the family, especially one with a measure of dysfunction, can be very upsetting for clients.

WARNING: If clients are dealing with major issues involving their childhood family, such as abuse, it is best to avoid this activity until they have sufficient internal resources to cope with the result.

Theory

Psychological games are common in families. You are in a game when you are in a conversation that seems familiar and you know that you and the other person will both end up feeling bad. Family members take up positions of Victim, Rescuer and Persecutor on the Drama Triangle (Karpman, 1968) and keep moving around it. The game can be stopped when a family member, perhaps through this sandtray activity, steps off the Drama Triangle and on to the Winner's Triangle (Choy, 1990). The Victim changes to being Vulnerable; the Rescuer becomes Caring; and the Persecutor changes to become Assertive.

Being in the middle

Invite clients to divide the sandtray into three sections. The central section represents the client at his/her ideal in the here-and-now. One of the sections is then created with negative influences from childhood that may be affecting the client today. The other shows negative influences from parental figures that have had an impact on the client's achieving the ideal shown in the middle section.

Once the sandtray is complete there are a couple of options, depending on the client's needs. One is to explore with clients ways in which they can strengthen the boundaries on each side so that the ideal in the middle is not hindered by negative influences from either side.

Another way of working with this sandtray is to encourage clients to see what positive elements in the sections on either side can be incorporated into the middle section to strengthen and expand it, thus reducing the negative influences from the section on either side.

In both cases invite clients to take a step back at each stage so that they can observe what they have created and consider what further action needs doing in the sandtray.

Theory

This sandtray can be understood in terms of the structural Parent, Adult and Child ego states. Sometimes there is a partial merging of ego states that Eric Berne described as 'contaminations'. He identified the mixture between Parent and Adult of a person as *delusions,* 'ideas imposed on him by his parents, which are so ingrown that he thinks they are part of his Real Self' (Berne, 1972/1975a, page 184). The area between the Adult and the Child he called *illusions,* 'ideas from his Child that he accepts as Adult and rational and tries to justify as such' (op cit).

Today these areas, shown as overlapping ego states, are known simply as *contaminations.* This sandtray can be seen as helping clients develop clear boundaries in their Adult ego state through a process of *decontamination.*

In Cocreative TA the Child and Parent ego states are seen as archaic and the Adult is described as *integrating.* Keith Tudor describes this as 'the individual's capacity to reflect upon and integrate their own archaic states as well as past introjects, and to draw on them in the service of present-centred relating – in life as well as in the therapeutic milieu, whether as therapist or client' (Tudor, 2003, page 202).

When clients take positive elements from their archaic Parent and Child ego states and place them in the middle section they are effectively symbolising an expanding Adult ego state.

Team work

Sandtray can be used effectively in working with groups as well as with individuals.

This sandtray exercise can be used to explore dynamics within a group. It is ideal for a group of between three and eight people who are not related or in an intimate relationship.

Invite the participants to choose objects to represent their relationships with each other and place them in the sandtray. This can be done either silently or by the participants discussing together their ideas as they choose and place the objects.

Once the objects are in place, the therapist invites the participants to look at the objects and their relationship with each other. Is there anything in the sandtray they would like to change and can agree on together? They make the changes by moving the objects and then look again. They can then consider further changes, and so on until they are satisfied with the result.

When any changes have been made and completed the therapist then asks them to give comments about the sandtray in terms of their thinking, feeling and intuition.

Theory

It is important to recognise, as John Dunne put it, that: 'No man is an island entire of itself; every man is a piece of the continent, a part of the main.' In the same way, no one is totally an individual; we are all part of a system. That system might be a place of work, a collection of friends or a therapy group.

Denton Roberts (1975) describes this in terms of circular boundaries, starting with the individual at the centre and progressing through gender, family, ethnic and cultural boundaries. Human beings are under constant pressure from socially induced stresses. These stresses, Denton writes, 'encourage people to make and remake decisions about themselves, and to write scripts which, though social, are as limiting as individual "life scripts"' (Denton, 1975, page 183). He concludes: 'Cultural, ethnic, sexual, family, social class and provincial scripts interlock with the personal life scripts, and both must be dealt with to achieve personal autonomy' (Denton, 1975, 189).

A new direction

Get clients to place various objects in the sandtray to show an aspect of themselves that they would like to change. Invite them to choose the objects intuitively, without thinking much about what they choose.

Once they are satisfied with what the sandtray looks like, invite clients to move the objects to create the change or new direction they would like in themselves. Again, suggest they do this intuitively.

Once they have done this talk together about what the new direction or change is like. As the therapist you may decide to suggest moving objects to new positions and seeing how it impacts on the client. Remember, though, that it is the client not the therapist who moves or touches the objects in the sandtray.

Theory

This activity is based on the fact that during childhood we all decide how we are going to be. We are not aware of our choice at the time but we live it out for the rest of our lives until we decide to change. The choices we make in response to the environment around us make up what we call life-script or, as it is often called, script.

What this exercise involves is to help clients tell their script story nonverbally and then decide if they want to change parts of it. By the time a child is seven, most of the main script issues are already in place. These include how they are going to cope in the world, how they relate to others and how they react in difficult situations. The decisions are made largely out of awareness. Sandtray therapy can help them change negative aspects of those decisions without words and effectively out of awareness.

When clients decide to change a negative aspect of their script it involves a redecision, which is a 'replacement of a self-limiting early decision by a new decision that takes account of the individual's full adult resources' (Stewart &

Joines, 1987 page 333). Suggest that clients observe in the coming days and weeks whether or not it becomes a new way of being.

Giving yourself permissions

Below is a list of negative 'Don't' messages, some of which clients receive from parents and other significant adults in childhood. Show or read to clients the list of Don't messages. Invite them to choose one of these negative messages that seems familiar to them and create it in the sandtray.

When they have finished, discuss the contents of the sandtray with them. Then ask them to use intuition in finding ways to change the contents to give them the permission they need (see the permission to the left of the Don't message).

When they have done this, talk about it together. Over the coming weeks work together to reinforce these permissions and counter any influence from the archaic Don't message.

Theory

As we grow through childhood we all develop negative messages that affect how we respond to the world around us. Bob and Mary Goulding called these 'Don't' messages injunctions (Goulding & Goulding, 1976). Pearl Drago's award winning work seeks to turn these into positive permissions that we can give ourselves in the here-and-now.

Permissions and Injunctions

Permission to exist	to preserve life	Don't exist
Permission to be oneself	to be one's sex	Don't be you
Permission to be a child	to have joy in life	Don't be a child
Permission to grow	to be one's age	Don't grow up
Permission to make it	to succeed	Don't succeed
Permission to be important	to have a sense of self-worth	Don't be important
Permission to be close	to trust	Don't be close
Permission to belong	to have a place, and a people	Don't belong
Permission to be well	to be healthy	Don't be well
Permission to be sane	to be in touch with reality	Don't be sane
Permission to think	to express thoughts	Don't think
Permission to feel	to express feelings safely	Don't feel

*Permission to be holy	to be spiritual	Don't be holy
*Permission to fight for justice	to take a stand	Don't stand up for justice

* Extra permissions/injunctions identified by Pearl Drago for the culture she works with in India

adapted from Pearl Drago (2004). *Happy Family: Parenting through family rituals.* Bombay: Alfreruby Publishers. The material itself is copyright © 1994 Pearl Drago

Relating with others

TA is based on three philosophical assumptions:

'People are OK.
Everyone has the capacity to think.
People decide their own destiny, and these decisions can be changed' (Stewart & Joines, 1987, page 6).

In this exercise clients are asked to divide their sandtray in two. On one side they depict themselves using a variety of objects. On the other side they choose someone else that they don't feel OK about right now, current or past, and depict that person in the sand. It could be a family relationship, a friend, a colleague at work or even a past enemy.

When they have finished, talk together about what they have created. Then invite them to decide, if they are willing, how they want to change their sandtray so that the other person is OK in relation to them.

When they have completed this second stage discuss what has been created and see what clients think and feel about the result.

Theory

Right from the beginning, TA has emphasised that there are four life positions (see, for instance, Stewart & Joines, 1987, page 120):

I'm OK, You're OK – healthy position
I'm OK, You're not OK – paranoid position
I'm not OK, You're OK – depressive position
I'm not OK, You're not OK – futility position

The ideal is the I'm OK, You're OK position. This does not mean that we always agree with the other person but that we accept them despite the differences.

Will clients only move on if they, for instance, forgive abusers and others who have messed up their lives? We certainly do not believe that. In our view when a client establishes an I'm OK, You're OK position towards others it can unnerve them and even compel them to 'deal with the internal disease that is robbing them (and others) of true beauty' (Allender & Longman, 1992).

The me I like, the me I don't like

In all human beings there are parts of who we are that we like and parts we don't like. This activity involves clients putting these two aspects in the sandtray and exploring any aspects of the two sides they have in common.

Invite them to divide the sandtray into two parts (not necessarily two equal halves). They then use objects to put on one side things about themselves that they like and on the other side things about themselves that they don't like.

As therapist ensure that you watch clients' facial expressions as this can be a powerful exercise, especially when clients are given 'permission' to portray the side of themselves that they don't like (sometimes thought of by clients as their 'bad' side).

When clients have finished the task ask them how they think and feel as they look at the two sides of themselves.

The next stage is for them to consider ways to link the two sides of the sandtray. This can be done through looking at objects that may be similar on each side or finding ways to bridge the two sides. Clients may need support and encouragement as they engage in this aspect of the exercise.

Finally, invite clients to look at any changes they have made and say how they now think and feel.

Theory

This activity assists clients in exploring their negative side and possibly finding positive elements even within that part. It is about our clients' admitting the mean, selfish side and finding positive aspects of that part of themselves.

Carl Jung explained this in terms of the archetypes Self and Shadow. The Self consists of aspects of the personality that are integrated and the Shadow contains aspects that are denied.

Similarly, Fritz Perls, founder of gestalt psychotherapy, used the term 'Topdog versus Underdog'. Topdog represents societal demands on the person while Underdog stands for the person's internal sabotage.

The equivalent in TA could be seen as a conflict between the positive aspects of the Adult ego state and the negative aspects of the Child: 'Psychoanalytic cure in structural terms means deconfusion of the Child with a largely decontaminated Adult as a therapeutic ally' (Berne, 1961/1975b, page 162).

Hargaden & Sills (2005) take this to an earlier developmental stage, looking at the Parent (P1), Adult (A1) and Child (C1) within the Child (C2) ego state. They explore the competing aspects of self in the infant (P1+/P1- and A1+/A1-), finding ways to integrate the self and thus deconfuse the Child ego state.

Parental influences

Invite clients to place objects in the sandtray to represent grown-ups and older children who had a significant influence on them in their early childhood. Consider prompting them with ideas such as parents, grandparents, uncles and aunts, teachers, carers and other adults who had an impact on them.

When they have completed the task ask them to look at the sandtray and to say what is their overall thinking and feeling. They may or may not want to talk about some or all of the objects. If they decide to talk be aware of any changes in their facial expressions as they do so.

Ask them if there is any object they would like to move in relation to the others. When they have done this ask them what it is like looking at the sandtray now. There may be several objects the person wants to move in this way before they are ready to stop.

This exercise looks at the structure of the Parent ego state in clients. A few people may find this exercise extremely distressing because they recognise they have few or even no positive parental influences. They may therefore need to work towards integrating in their Parent ego state positive Parent messages from various people they know now or in the past. Then they can create a more positive Parent ego state. This can be done verbally or through placing objects in the sandtray to represent the positive messages of the other people and exploring how they can embrace these messages for themselves.

Theory

This exercise in based on the structural model of ego states. In this the Parent ego state is formed from the thoughts, feelings and behaviours of Parents and significant other figures (adults and older children). These influences from parents and other adults are 'swallowed whole'. Because of this they are often known as introjects. For more on this see Stewart, Ian, & Joines (1987), pages 30-38.

Clients can explore in the sand aspects of parents and significant others who have been used in their childhood to develop their Parent ego state.

Moving the objects around is a way of beginning to shift Parental influences to reduce the toxic effect of negative messages and to give more prominence to positive Parent messages.

The second stage of introducing symbols to represent other people with a more positive Parent ego state is part of what is known as Spot Reparenting (Osne, 1974).

My Child the hero

Invite clients to use intuition in deciding several ages of their childhood. Usually significant positive or negative things happened for them at those ages. Clients may not remember those events but they are likely to know the ages.

Once clients have decided the ages (writing them down if necessary), invite them to choose a variety of objects to represent each age. Group them in the sandtray according to that age.

When clients have finished, consider discussing together each age. Keep your language in the third person. Help clients to identify the positive resources that helped the child at that age to survive and get their needs met. Support clients in recognising that at each stage the child represented was a hero to them.

Theory

This activity is based on the Child ego state, defined as 'a set of behaviours, thoughts and feelings which are replayed from the individual's own childhood' (Stewart & Joines, 1987, page 327). As therapists we often think of the Child ego state in fairly negative ways. This exercise focuses on the positive resources the literal child at different stages used to cope with whatever he or she was facing at the time. In that sense each of us has, at different ages in childhood, several heroes who helped us survive and get our needs met.

John Bradshaw, who originally used TA in his therapeutic work, encourages people to find their inner wounded child at a particular age and champion that child as the hero, or wonder child, who did things in the best way he or she could.

Bradshaw writes: 'As you champion your wounded child, he comes to trust you and your nourishing protection; he knows that you will not abandon him. That deep sense of safety and basic trust allows the wonder child to emerge.

Then, to be yourself, requires no work or effort' (Bradshaw, 1990, page 256).

Involvement

Empathy does not have to be confined only to face-to-face contact with your clients. Sandtray can be used for you – and your client – to experience genuine empathy while looking at the plastic, metal and natural objects in the sand. Then, together, you can go beyond empathy to *involvement.* This is based on a relational approach known as Contact-in-Relationship.

Invite clients to do a sandtray about a difficult time in their life. Track them carefully as they develop the sandtray. Be prepared to comment if you observe difficult or distressing emotions as they progress.

When they have finished the sandtray discuss together the start of the process (Enquiry). Together seek to enter the sandtray figures' world. As therapist attempt through Enquiry to experience the impact on you of what has happened to the figures/objects in the sandtray. Encourage your client to experience empathy for the figures, even if one or more of them represents themselves.

Then move on to Attunement. Adjust your wording so that as you talk with your clients you feel in tune with the emotional needs of the sandtray figures.

Finally, move into Involvement. Let the story of the figures in the sandtray impact you, going beyond empathy. Help your clients to feel that depth of empathy for the figures as well.

Theory

Richard Erskine, whose team at the Institute for Integrative Psychotherapy, New York, has developed Contact-in-Relationship (see Erskine, et al, 1999), believes it is important for therapists to show genuine Involvement with clients. This may need to be done by moving to sit near the client in the therapy room or making a phone call to clients between sessions.

He writes: 'The therapist's willingness to initiate interpersonal contact or to take responsibility for a major share of the therapeutic work normalises the client's relational need to have someone else put energy into reaching out to him or her. Such action communicates to the client that the therapist is involved in the relationship' (Erskine, 2002, page 9).

My support system

For this activity invite your clients to depict themselves in the centre of the sand. Suggest that they include their qualities, hopes and interests. The second stage is to create their support system radiating from the centre. If clients have difficulty in knowing what their support system involves, you might prompt them with words such as family, friends, work colleagues, clubs/groups and internet social networks.

When your clients have created their support system talk to them about what they see in the sandtray. What do they feel and think about the support system they have shown?

The final stage is for clients to make changes in the sandtray, if needed. Once this is done discuss again the support system they have created.

Theory

People have certain fundamental needs or hungers. Eric Berne (1975a) identified three hungers that he believed all human beings have. They are:

Stimulus (or sensation) hunger – the need for mother-child attachment.

Recognition hunger – the need to receive strokes (units of recognition).

Structure hunger – the desire people have to structure their lives, work, entertainment, etc.

Tony White has added the notion of attachment hunger, 'a biological, psychological and social hunger for an attachment to a caretaking figure'. He writes: 'This hunger persists throughout our lives. However, from adolescence onward, peer attachments allow the childhood need for a parental attachment to decrease . . . without at least one firm and secure attachment in adulthood there is also mental and physical decline' (White, 1997, page 303).

This sandtray activity enables clients to explore the satisfaction or otherwise of their hungers, particularly for attachment, and to make new decisions about how these hungers can be fulfilled.

Four feelings

This sandtray is an exploration of the four feelings: sadness, anger, scare and joy. Encourage clients to divide the sandtray into four sections and to create one of these feelings in each.

Once the sandtray is complete, discuss what clients have created in the four sections. Does the client have a preferred feeling? What feeling was not encouraged as clients were growing up, either within their family or in their culture generally? For instance, in English and Welsh cultures anger is generally repressed.

Clients may want to expand this sandtray in subsequent sessions, exploring a particular feeling in the whole sandtray, perhaps even the one or two feelings clients were discouraged from expressing when they were in childhood.

Theory

This activity is based on the four 'authentic' feelings named in TA as mad, sad, scared and glad. Other feelings (jealousy, embarrassment, guilt etc) are often used to cover up the authentic feelings. These are known as racket feelings and are part of the racket (or script) system developed by Erskine & Zalcman (1979).

A racket feeling has been defined as 'a familiar emotion, learned and encouraged in childhood, experienced in many different stress situations, and maladaptive as an adult means of problem-solving' (Stewart & Joines, 1987, page 209).

Roger Day, writing for young children, says about racket feelings: 'We have cover-up feelings, such as jealousy and loneliness, so we do not have to show or deal with how we really feel. Cover-up feelings leave us feeling bad or confused . . . It is best to show your real feelings so people can understand you and help you' (Day, 2004, page 5).

Creating the four feelings in the sand can be a first step for clients in exploring and expressing their real (authentic) feelings.

Family constellation

Invite clients to choose objects to represent a constellation of their family members and place them in the sandtray in relation to each other.

Once clients have finished, ask them if there are others missing from the sandtray. In this exercise it is important that everyone in the family is included, past and present. Some may be left out because they caused problems, abused someone or were in prison. Others might have died. Encourage clients to include them all, including still births, abortions, miscarriages.

The next stage is to look at the constellation, the position of family members and their relationship to each other. Ask clients questions to ensure you understand the dynamics of the family.

Finally, using your own intuition, invite clients to move objects in relation to the other objects. Clients may come up with their own ideas. After each move stop and observe the sandtray. What has changed in the dynamics? Keep encouraging a moving of the objects until clients seem ready to stop.

Theory

This sandtray is based on the work of German psychotherapist Bert Hellinger. He developed Family & Systemic Constellations, drawing on the influence of Eric Berne (1010-1970) and TA as well as Psychodrama, developed by Romanian-born Jacob Levy Moreno (1889-1974).

Hellinger, now in his late 80s, continues his approach by inviting members of the audience to recreate the client's family, then moving them around in relation to each other.

He strongly believes that, for healing to become effective, everyone needs to be included in a constellation, even those who have been excluded because of crime or abuse. He says: 'In the end all in the family are equal. Nobody is better, nobody is worse. So at the end, we can be very humble and take our place in our family, and by taking our right place in our family we feel good and free' (Hellinger, 2001).

References

Allender, Dan, & Longman, Tremper (1992). *Bold Love.* Colorado Springs: NavPress.

Ammann, Ruth (1991). *Healing and Transformation in Sandplay: Creative processes made visible.* La Salle, Illinois: Open Court.

Axline, Virginia (1974). *Play Therapy.* New York: Ballantine Books. (Original work published 1948.)

Axline, Virginia (1990). *Dibs: In search of self.* London: Penguin. (Original work published 1964.)

Berne, Eric (1949). The nature of intuition. *Psychiatric Quarterly, 23,* pages 203-226.

Berne, Eric (1975a). *What Do You Say After You Say Hello?* London: Corgi. (Original work published 1972.)

Berne, Eric (1975b). *Transactional Analysis in Psychotherapy.* London: Souvenir Press. (Original work published 1961.)

Bradshaw, John (1990). *Homecoming: Reclaiming and championing your inner child.* New York: Bantam Books.

Carey, Lois (2008). *Sandplay Therapy with Children and Families.* Lanham, Maryland: Rowman & Littlefield. (Original work published 1999.)

Choy, Acey (1990). The winner's triangle. *Transactional Analysis Journal, 20,* 1, pages 40-46.

Day, Roger (2004). *Being Mad, Being Glad.* Oxford: Raintree Publishers.

Drago, Pearl (2004). *Happy Family: Parenting through family rituals.* Bombay: Alfreruby Publishers.

Erskine, Richard, & Zalcman, MJ (1979). The racket system: A model for racket analysis. *Transactional Analysis Journal, 9,* pages 51-59.

Erskine, Richard, Moursund, JP & Trautman, Rebecca (1999). *Beyond Empathy: A theory of contact-in-relationship.* Philadelphia: Brunner/Mazel.

Erskine, Richard (2002). Relational needs. *EATA Newsletter, 73,* February 2002, pages 5-9.

Fowlie, Heather (2010). The process of relating: The key to growth and change. *The Psychotherapist, 46,* Autumn 2010, pages 15-16.

Gladwell, Malcolm (2005). *Blink: The power of thinking without thinking.* London: Penguin Books.

Goulding, Robert, & Goulding, Mary (1976). Injunctions, decisions and redecisions. *Transactional Analysis Journal, 6,* 1, pages 41-48.

Hargaden & Sills, (2005). Deconfusion of the Child ego state: A relational perspective, in Cornell, William, & Hargaden, Helena, *From Transactions to Relations: The emergence of a relational tradition in transactional analysis,* Chadlington, Oxfordshire: Haddon Press (pages 155 to 178).

Hellinger, Bert (2001). *Introduction to Family Constellations.* Lecture and demonstration in Taipei.

ISFT (Institute for Solution-Focused Therapy) (2012). World wide web: www.solutionfocused.net

Karpman, Stephen (1968). Fairy tales and script drama analysis. *Transactional Analysis Bulletin. 7,* 26, pages 39-43.

Knell, Susan (1995). *Cognitive Behavioural Play Therapy.* Blue Ridge Summit, Pennsylvania: Jason Aronson.

Lowenfeld, Margaret (1993). *Understanding children's sandplay: Lowenfeld's world technique.* UK: Antony Rowe Ltd. (Original work published 1979 as *The World Technique.*)

Oaklander, Violet (1997). The therapeutic process with children and adolescents. *Gestalt Review, 1,* 4, pages 292-317.

Osne, Russell (1974). Spot reparenting. *Transactional Analysis Journal 4,* 3, pages 40-46.

Roberts, Denton (1975). *Transactional Analysis Journal 5,* 1 January 1975, pages 183-9)

Stewart, Ian (1996). *Developing Transactional Analysis Counselling.* London: Sage.

Stewart, Ian, & Joines, Vann (1987). *TA Today: A new introduction to transactional analysis.* Nottingham: Lifespace Publishing.

Tudor, Keith (2003). The neopsyche: The integrating Adult ego state, in *Ego States,* edited by Charlotte Sills & Helena Hargaden, London: Worth Publishing.

Turner, Barbara (2005). *The Handbook of Sandplay Therapy.* Cloverdale, California: Temenos Press.

Wells, Herbert George (H G) (1911). *Floor Games.* Public domain.

West, Janet (1992). *Child-Centred Play Therapy.* London: Edward Arnold.

White, Tony (1997). Symbiosis and attachment hunger. *Transactional Analysis Journal, 27,* 4, pages 300-304.

Yasenik, Lorri, & Gardner, Ken (2012). *Play Therapy Dimensions Model: A decision-making guide for integrative play therapists.* London: Jessica Kingsley. (Original work published 2004.)

CPSIA information can be obtained
at www.ICGtesting.com
Printed in the USA
LVHW022347291120
672987LV00016B/1786